When Relationships Hurt...

I write & color

A devotional journal & coloring book
Created to foster healing

By Jandre

Copyright © 2019 by Jandre

All rights reserved, including the right to reproduce this book or portions thereof in any form whatsoever. For information, please email: judie@jandrencompany.com

For information about special discounts for bulk purchases or for speaking engagements, please contact: judie@jandrencompany.com
Manufactured in the United States of America

Scriptures quotations in this book are NIV. Scripture quotations marked (NIV) are taken from the Holy Bible, New International Version, NIV. Copyright 1973, 1978, 1984, 2011 by Biblicea, Inc. Used by permission by Zondervan. All rights reserved worldwide. Www.zondervan.com, the "NIV" and the "New International Version" are trademarks registered in the United states Patent and Trademark office by Biblica, Inc.

Cover Artwork design by Elizabeth Hunt
Editing by: Beyond Wordz
Illustrations by LaSquizzie Kern

Library of Congress Cataloging in Publication has been applied for:
ISBN 978-1-7336126-0-9

Dedication

With wholehearted love to my Abba Father whose constant guard over me and continued guidance has kept me through life's many circumstances.

With amazing grace and love to my mom, sisters, and friends, you know who you are, you all are my circle, keeping me consistently committed to bettering myself.

And with thanksgiving and love to my husband and two daughters. Thank you for giving me room to grow both loudly and quietly. I am humbled to share space with you all; you all are my bubble.

Table of Contents

Dedication	iii
Prelude to the Introduction	vi
Introduction: Me, Myself And, Oh, The Relationships I Have	vii
People Make The World Go 'Round	1
Something Happened. I'm Trying To Work This Out	5
When Hope Turns To Grief And Happiness To Sadness	9
How Did We Get Here?	13
I Can't Believe Your Behavior Toward Me	17
Can We Work Through This Together?	21
This Is Affecting Me More Than I Realized!	25
Wow, You're Gone. Did You Care For Me?	29
God, Do You Want Me In This Much Pain?	33
Who Is Going To Take Care Of Me?	37
Pride Says, "Why Should I Make The First Move?"	41
I'm Angry, Resentful And Bitter	45
Helpers Along The Way	49
A Process Toward Reconciliation	53
I Surrender. I Am Going To Cooperate With Your Plan	57
Your Presence Is Like A Balm	61
Back To Life, Back To Reality	65
Your Love, O'lord, Is Amazing	69
It Didn't Turn Out As Planned. Now What?	73
Look At Me! I Feel Like I Have Wings!	77
About the Author	81

Prelude to the Introduction

"Above all, love each other deeply, because love covers over a multitude of sins."

1 Peter 4:8

Introduction:
Me, Myself And, Oh, The Relationships I Have

Relationships. We all have them, be it with family, friends, colleagues, associates, and of course, the relationships we work hard to either ignore or avoid, like with an estranged sibling or an enemy.

Relationships are the living acts or actions taken to relate with others for a purpose and goal. Furthermore, relationships are meant to solidify a common ground or foundation, to reinforce a vision and to embrace differences to find commonality with another person(s).

God created us to have loving relationships—first, of course, with Him as our Father and Creator, but also with each other. This plan from God is perfect, yet it can be difficult to sustain. God's multi-faceted blessing in giving us relationships helps us to develop and mature to be more loving, fruitful, giving, positive and thriving human beings. Without good relationships, we compromise our capacity to be godly and great.

As we look around in our society, there seems to be a lingering theme and full support for that old adage of "Me, myself and I" or "I can do bad all by myself." Being alone and independent is celebrated. There are times to be in solitude for our well-being and growth. However, working independently at all times is not how we were intended to live. We are and were intended to live in community, not in isolation from others. "No man is an island." No one was created to be alone, although, with the recent global pandemic, many people were forced into long-term isolation. Loneliness was literally experienced both by people living with others as well as those living without. While some people used the time to reflect on their purpose, goals and fostering better relationships, others succumbed to the loneliness and were left severely depressed, despaired, and hopeless, thereby crippling or deterring them from destiny and fruitfulness. This is not God's good plan.

Relationships can be difficult to sustain when hurts are inflicted. In this special devotional coloring book, I want to offer you tools—thought nuggets that are good and godly to consider, especially when various hurts assault you in your relationships. You can creatively, prayerfully and strategically navigate out of the pain of being hurt and get onto the tarmac of thriving and the process of winning. Have the joy God intentioned for you despite the quality of relationships you have.

Does this mean you will have a kumbaya story in all your relationships? Will your world suddenly turn into this utopian atmosphere where everyone gets along? Will there never be a hurt again? The answer is a resounding no! People will always come and go. There is a time and a season for all things under the sun, but what if you were meant to endure longer with that girlfriend, make that phone call to that colleague, learn something from that cousin or heal that mother you abandoned. Was that divorce really necessary? Too many of us are aborting relationships that God intended for our good. Many of us are letting go and running away when it's not necessary. The enemy comes to steal, kill and destroy. Could he be the one gloating over you instead of God's glory? As you go through this book, my greatest prayer is that love rather than hurt would determine who and why we have or do not have in our relationship circles.

Words of Reflection

Chapter 1

People Make The World Go 'Round

There is a relationship theory that believes people are separated from another person by six degrees. The theory states the idea that all people, on average, are six or fewer social connections away from each other. Whether this is true or not, I cannot say, but I do know for sure that we are all children of our creator, and if he is the head and we are the body, aren't we all supposed to naturally get along?

Living in peace and having good will toward our neighbors and friends should be our pursuit. Yet, the reality is, just as with the body where your hand may be able to reach your foot, but you can't seem to scratch your back unless you have help or an extension, the same dynamic exists in people. Our differences are meant to complement us, humble us and teach us. Life's journey will present us with various struggles, different ideologies, cultural shocks and difficult encounters, yet the challenge is to find what connects us. What is the extension?

Some would say, "You stay in your lane, and I will stay in mine," or "What is the benefit of accepting your difference?" As you consider the people or groups of people in your life, ask yourself if there is a balanced exchange of give and take? Are virtues of honor and respect being held up? Are you doing to others as you would have them do to you? Are the relationships positive or negative, godly or ungodly? Not everyone you meet will add value to your life, but do not underestimate the value you may bring to the lives of others.

God desired that we all live in peace with one another. Do not reject those different than you.

Ephesians 4:25 "Therefore each of you must put off falsehood and speak truthfully to your neighbor, for we are all members of one body."

John 15:15 "I no longer call you servants, because a servant does not know his master's business. Instead, I have called you friends, for everything that I learned from my Father I have made known to you."

Matthew 5:14-16 "You are the light of the world. A town built on a hill cannot be hidden. Neither do people light a lamp and put it under a bowl. Instead, they put it on its stand, and it gives light to everyone in the house. In the same way, let your light shine before others, that they may see your good deeds and glorify your Father in heaven."

Words of Reflection

Chapter 2

Something Happened. I'm Trying To Work This Out

The bumps in the road. Let's call them friction, arguments, challenges, disappointments, betrayals, misunderstandings, deceptions and all the like. You will know there is a bump when conversations run differently or take on a different tone. It could be a frantic call or when there is "no more hanging out" with people you use to hang out with in the past. Some events cause you to freeze or pause.

Trials, hardships and challenges are part of life's process. Things can go awry and leave us feeling whiplashed in bewilderment. There are times you see them coming and there are times you do not, so what do you do? Are you one of those people who will usually dive right in during a circumstance and become the savior-helper, or the fix-it kind of a person? Would you consider yourself to be the frozen-still type? There's also the runner, the one who dodges or who goes off alone. Surely some reactions can lead you further away from peace, no matter how you try to avoid them.

God cares about you and who you are in relationship with, at all times. He can empower you with guidance. He wants to heal and help you every step of the way. Every child of God has an advocate in Him—the Holy Spirit, also known as the Wonderful Counselor. Certain life bumps don't have to derail you or cause you delay. Rather, they can serve as reminders to turn to your counselor, your helper to grow. Some circumstances remind you of your resilience, growth and strength. Make declarations that you will thrive, have success and victory through the Savior!

Proverbs 3:5-6 "Trust in the Lord with all your heart and lean not on your own understanding; in all your ways submit to him, and he will make your paths straight."

John 16:33 "I have told you these things, so that in me you may have peace. In this world you will have trouble. But take heart! I have overcome the world."

Hebrews 13:5 "Keep your lives free from the love of money and be content with what you have, because God has said, "Never will I leave you; never will I forsake you."

Words of Reflection

Chapter 3

When Hope Turns To Grief And Happiness To Sadness

    Businesses have marketplace trends that come and go. Like fads coming and going, the timespan can be unpredictable, setting budgets and performance predictions off the charts. Relationships will also cause you to navigate through awesome life changes and through some real messy ones. These seasons can appear abruptly, and how long they last is not always up to us.

    Moments of volatility require being focused. There are forces of evil that may exist against you. There are also powers of evil persuasion that may be beyond your control to manage. When trials appear overwhelming, pray, find your tribe and be honest with yourself. In Christ, hope is never lost but is always. During the pandemic months, many people encountered difficult times; some whose sorrows are too dismal to talk about. Yet, moments of change started to occur, and what appeared as a loss resulted in stories of gain, rebounding, overcoming, resilience and victory.

    The mystery and reality of suffering are often not talked about. The soul is never really prepared for pain, disappointment or discouragement; that makes you human. Be prepared. Rainy days will come, but they don't have to drown you. Have a plan and understand trouble doesn't always last. Take comfort in knowing your heavenly Father promises to be near the brokenhearted (Ps 34:18), and He sent us a comforter that will be with us always. (Jn 14:16 & 26). To rebound in a more holistic way will require prayer, being patient, reach out to your trusted tribe for support. Have self-honesty because a pure heart will see the Lord.

Ecclesiastes 3:1 "There is a time for everything, and a season for every activity under the heavens."

1 Peter 5:8 "Be alert and of a sober mind. Your enemy the devil prowls around like a roaring lion looking for someone to devour."

Proverbs 4:23 "Above all else, guard your heart, for everything you do flows from it."

Words of Reflection

Chapter 4

How Did We Get Here?

Like a historian, or maybe an archaeologist at work, there may be times our own efforts to understand things from the past can take a life of its own. While it is natural and healthy to evaluate your current state to determine the wise step forward, beware however of living in the past. Trying to piece together a story that is at most sensible or at least still full of unknown answers can become a job.

Be careful when the thoughts of reflection become negative. Do any of the following thoughts sound familiar?

- I thought we were connected.
- We had a lot in common, and the relationship was very engaging.
- I can't believe how disconnected we have been.
- Boy, we neglected to serve and love each other.
- I remember the good old days.
- Was I too controlling, or did my freedom cause you to drift away from me?

There is danger in casting unfounded or imbalanced blame on others. Being overly critical and condemning is not healthy. It is equally unhealthy to harbor all the faults oneself and become self-condemning. Sure, the reality of losing self-control or forfeiting valuable convictions can hurt and present us with real pain. Let the past serve as a good teacher that is on your side to lead you into success for God's glory. Your job is to understand the past and harness the courage to face a new day better because living in the past is dangerous. Ultimately, healing requires understanding the grace of God and our human nature. Our human nature will fight against what God wants but pursue life on God's terms and live by His spirit. Be careful of the coulda, shoulda, woulda talk can result in thoughts of regret, and that is not a healthy solution.

Self-reflection and practicing introspection to see where, what and how you contribute to your relationship dynamics is a good practice. Do this with helpful resources like therapy, meditation and prayer.

Proverbs 4:23 "Above all else, guard your heart, for everything you do flows from it."

Proverbs 14:12 "There is a way that appears to be right, but in the end, it leads to death."

Philippians 3:14 "I press on toward the goal to win the prize for which God has called me heavenward in Christ Jesus."

Words of Reflection

Chapter 5

I Can't Believe Your Behavior Toward Me

Because we live in a sinful world, we do face offenses that can cause bewilderment. It is not fair how some children are treated. It is not fair how some spouses treat one another. It is not fair how some bosses treat their colleagues. Sadly, life is not always fair.

Have you heard the saying? "Hurt people, hurt people," and while this at times is true, I believe as humans, we all carry a little hurt in ourselves. Understanding the pains that one feels can lead us to be empathic, sympathetic and humble. These attitudes are very important and oh how we should long have them in our wheelhouse. Having an attitude that fosters relatability in human relationships is Christlike. Being truthful about our hurt and weaknesses positions us for healing, freedom and strength. Being vulnerable at the right times invites others to open up and build trust. Make it your prayer to become better aware of our intentions and actions, thus becoming responsible for guarding our hearts and managing our character, then we can see clearly to help others.

Sometimes, we measure our value to other people using the wrong scale. For instance, we sometimes consider all we have done physically to help the other person instead of using scales that measure the quality of our character in the relationship. In other words, did I give you something, or did I give you myself, my time and my attention? To our friends and colleagues, we might appear to be the champion, but to your closest relationship partner, who are you, and who do you say you are?

<u>Mark 8:27</u> "Jesus and his disciples went on to the villages around Caesarea Philippi. On the way, he asked them, 'Who do people say I am?'"

<u>Matthew 7:1-5</u> "Do not judge, or you too will be judged. For in the same way you judge others, you will be judged, and with the measure you use, it will be measured to you. "Why do you look at the speck of sawdust in your brother's eye and pay no attention to the plank in your own eye? How can you say to your brother, 'Let me take the speck out of your eye,' when all the time there is a plank in your own eye? You hypocrite, first take the plank out of your own eye, and then you will see clearly to remove the speck from your brother's eye."

<u>Galatians 5:22-23</u> "But the fruit of the Spirit is love, joy, peace, forbearance, kindness, goodness, faithfulness, gentleness and self-control. Against such things there is no law."

Words of Reflection

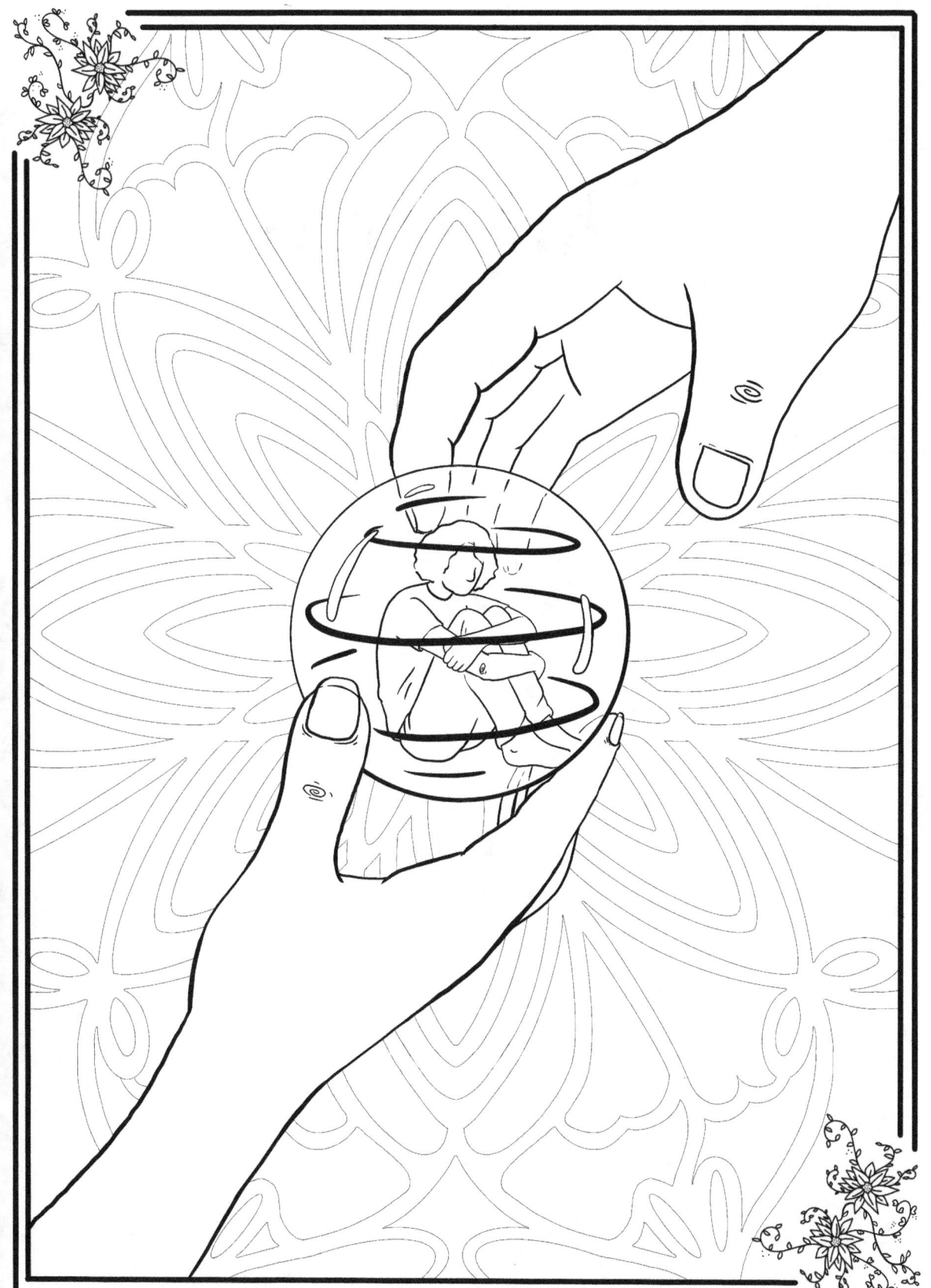

Chapter 6

Can We Work Through This Together?

So, are you ready to move toward harmony in a relationship, but the other person is not ready?

- Do we need to see a counselor, a trusted friend, mediator, doctor, lawyer or minister?
- Hi, do you think we can meet? It's been a long time. I'm ready.
- Do we need to seek professional help?
- How about we pray together?
- We should devise a plan. Let's sit for a coffee or come up with a schedule.
- Can we talk, maybe have sex, or just stare at each other?
- Do you realize I'm right here? Can you look at me?
- Hi, I'm calling again. I'll await your call back.
- I'm going to set the table for two. I hope you can make it tonight.
- Are you ignoring my texts? Hello?
- Let's just do something!

Re-connection or working on reconciliation, as beautiful as it is, can be awkward. Celebrate yourself in this hour because it takes love, courage, maturity and vision to work toward unity and peace especially in this very fragmented world.

Do not be dismayed in being first to initiate the process of reconciliation or healing in your relationships. Have a plan; successful outcomes oftentimes go through a process. Be patient. Complex situations require prayer, wisdom and a strategic plan. Remember, there are forces cheering you on, however, there are also forces against you.

As a destined victor, your responsibility is to seek direction. Life is a journey, not a sprint. Be patient in your attempts and do not rush the process. There may be times when space is needed. Peace is not associated with a timetable, but rather with an assurance that comes from being confident in whose you are, a child of the King.

Psalm 32:8 "I will instruct you and teach you in the way you should go; I will counsel you with my loving eye on you."

1 Corinthians 10:13 "No temptation has overtaken you except what is common to mankind. And God is faithful; he will not let you be tempted beyond what you can bear. But when you are tempted, he will also provide a way out so that you can endure it."

Ephesians 4:12 "So Christ himself gave the apostles, the prophets, the evangelists, the pastors and teachers to equip his people for works of service, so that the body of Christ may be built up."

Words of Reflection

Chapter 7

This Is Affecting Me More Than I Realized!

Be honest with yourself, how are you doing? How is your mental health? You owe it yourself and to those you love to be well. The impact of stress, compounded with disappointments or life's setbacks can take a toll on even the strongest of us. People have various ways of responding to disappointments, pain and trauma. Our souls absorb these things differently, however, the result can lead to anger, resentment, bitterness and mental and physical breakdowns.

Learning to be okay when you are not okay, is okay. Acknowledging your compromised state doesn't make you a failure—it is human and honest. Depending on the gravity of your circumstances, you may have to be a bit passive or a bit aggressive with getting help. Feeling sad, scared or lonely is normal when you experience a loss. Crying doesn't mean you are weak, and you don't need to protect your loved ones or friends by putting on a brave face. Showing your true feelings can be revealing enough to manifest the right help you may need. God sees and He also cares.

No one enjoys feeling as if the floor has dropped out from underneath them and that they are losing control. Fear arises because of uncertainty and doubt. Sometimes our efforts or lack thereof often leads to exhaustion. This is an indicator that we need to surrender. God's spirit can lead us in a way outside of our own strength for His glory.

It's not a good time to be alone when exhibiting thoughts of mental and physical distress. Pray in community if you are too weak. Journal, color, worship, exercise and love yourself! His strength is perfect in our weakness. Look to Him for healing. Proper counseling can help you determine which course of action can give you the best balance.

<u>Psalm 18:2</u> "The Lord is my rock, my fortress and my deliverer; my God is my rock, in whom I take refuge, my shield and the horn of my salvation, my stronghold."

<u>Psalm 32:8</u> "I will instruct you and teach you in the way you should go; I will counsel you with my loving eye on you."

<u>Psalm 91:1-2</u> "He who dwells in the secret place of the Most High shall abide under the shadow of the Almighty. I will say of the Lord, 'He is my refuge and my fortress; my God in Him I will trust.'"

Words of Reflection

Chapter 8

Wow, You're Gone. Did You Care For Me?

As infants, many of us were nursed and cared for by our parents, a single parent or guardians. In our innocence, we accepted their care, unaware of whether it was ok, good, perfect or excellent. We received care, whether it was out of love, duty, persuasion or choice. As with growth and maturity, knowledge and understanding come. We are now in a better place to judge or understand the level of care we received during our rearing years as adults.

Consider this same assessment of the care for your present relationships. Are you in the infant, teenage or adult stage of your relationship? While this is not a traditional way to view your relationship, give yourself the time to consider whether the value and care received is balanced. Was there a balanced exchange of love and sacrifice? Were there two adults in the relationship, or one adult and a child, or two teenagers?

The maturity God expects from his children is measured by the fruits of the spirit and wisdom, as well as the basic, everyday respect, integrity and dignity shared and given. Have you loved yourself as you were also to love others?

A loss should not always be reflective of what was taken from you but rather what is now gained. What is left in your treasure chest? If you are still alive, give God praise! Are you fulfilling your God-given purpose? Are you growing? Carry hope within you and go forward. You will not be disappointed!

Leviticus 19:18 "'Do not seek revenge or bear a grudge against anyone among your people but love your neighbor as yourself. I am the Lord."

Colossians 3:13 "Bear with each other and forgive one another if any of you has a grievance against someone. Forgive as the Lord forgave you."

1 Peter 4:8 "Above all, love each other deeply, because love covers over a multitude of sins."

Words of Reflection

Chapter 9

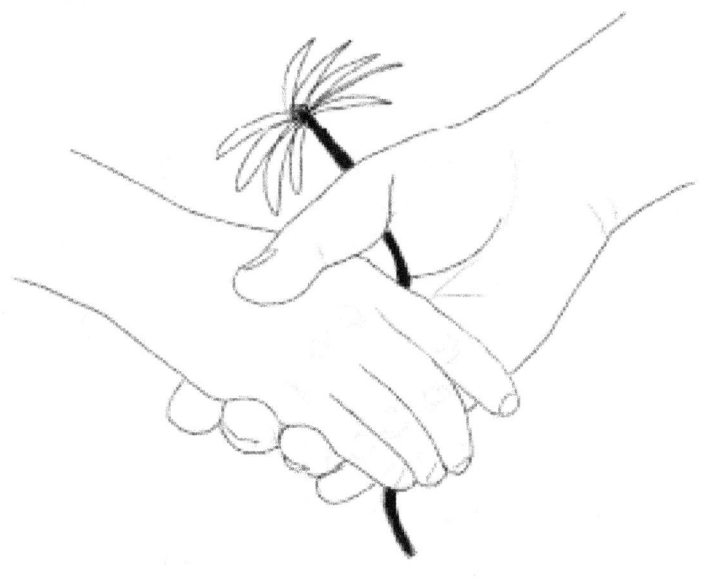

God, Do You Want Me In This Much Pain?

- Is there a good time for love to hurt? There is possibly no love in this relationship if it hurts this bad. Lord, do you see my hurt, my pain, my tears and my sufferings? Are you off today? I am all cried out now.
- I am supposed to be blessed, yet this feels like a curse.
- I was wronged, betrayed, rejected, misunderstood, humiliated, laughed at and abandoned.
- Am I not a good person? I don't deserve that treatment.
- Do you know who I am? I'm the son of so and so and the daughter of...
- I'm sophisticated, awarded, funny, put together, educated, accomplished, nice, busy and a good person. So, why is this happening to me?
- God, do you even see me? Do you even care?

Jesus could have called a whole troop of angels to rescue him before the crucifixion, but He did not. His purpose and mission kept him on course. There is a mystery to the pain and suffering that some of us endure, and unfortunately, the mystery of it may never unfold in this life. However, let's keep our minds on love, purpose and mission, as Christ did. You will be surprised how tears can turn to joy and mourning to laughter and dancing.

Yes, bad things do happen to good people. In these moments, do not self-condemn or cast judgment against God because he does see and care for you. Believe he is working all things out for your good. Some trials are intended to mature you, and just like growing pains, are meant to allow you to shed a part of that old self that needs to be gone. God transitions you out of your old seasons, no matter how challenging, and journeys with you to become someone new for his glory. Trust the process.

<u>John 16:33</u> "I have told you these things, so that in me you may have peace. In this world you will have trouble. But take heart! I have overcome the world."

<u>John 19:1-3</u> "Then Pilate took Jesus and had him flogged. The soldiers twisted together a crown of thorns and put it on his head. They clothed him in a purple robe and went up to him again and again, saying, 'Hail, king of the Jews!' And they slapped him in the face."

<u>1 Corinthians 13: 4-7</u> "Love is patient, love is kind. It does not envy, it does not boast, it is not proud. It does not dishonor others, it is not self-seeking, it is not easily angered, it keeps no record of wrongs. Love does not delight in evil but rejoices with the truth. It always protects, always trusts, always hopes, always perseveres."

Words of Reflection

Chapter 10

Who Is Going To Take Care Of Me?

Life sometimes may seem like a fast-moving train or as slow as a slug making its way down a tree. Through it all, we must show up, be present and responsible. Some of us fall off a routine and feel depressed. Others keep moving as if nothing phases them. Some quiet down and get reflective. Others drink tea or coffee and meditate, while others socialize and drink and drink. Some stay in the house all day, and others stroll in late at night. Is any extreme ever healthy?

With God, you do not have to be ruled by anxiety or inaction caused by depression. Instead, practice self-love habits, create a vision board, pick up a new sport or hobby, exercise, color, sing, dance, serve strangers and the people you love. Crave peace and be led forth in peace. Don't get lost in the whirlwind.

- What are you doing to take care of your soul?
- Do you agree with your soul's current passion and desires?
- Do those desires line up with God's plan for you?

The greatest person you can take care of, despite the challenges of the day is **YOU**. Do yourself a favor and trust your heavenly Father. Believe in His promises, which are sure and faithful. He cares for you deeply.

<u>Psalm 34:15</u> "The eyes of the Lord are on the righteous, and his ears are attentive to their cry."

<u>Hebrews 13:5</u> "Keep your lives free from the love of money and be content with what you have, because God has said, 'Never will I leave you; never will I forsake you.'"

<u>1 Peter 5:7</u> "Cast all your anxiety on him because he cares for you."

Words of Reflection

Chapter 11

Pride Says, "Why Should I Make The First Move?"

Beware of forces that promote division. Jesus once said, "He who is without sin can cast the first stone" (John 8:7). When it comes to living right, being right or saying the right thing, pray that we have an eagerness to have a lifestyle of righteousness. In essence, life is too short and unpredictable. Do you realize exercising forgiveness is a source of power and makes you powerful? It is often misunderstood, yet the act of humbly offering forgiveness gets God's attention quickly. It was forgiveness that God demonstrated toward us that offers this open door to a heavenly life and heavenly help.

Olympians train not to get to the starting line, but to win a medal. The obstacles and competition they face to get to the Olympics are undoubtedly challenging. As elite athletes, if they had not had the mindset of aiming to finish first in their local, state and national races, they would not have made it to the world stage. Working toward or maintaining a healthy relationship requires having a willingness for peaceful living and a desire for love and respect.

Harboring unforgiveness can lead to having ailments, both in the mind and body. Anxiety can take over either because of fear of the reaction of wanting to fix a broken fellowship or mend a misunderstanding, not knowing the outcome can result in stress. It's ok to have a game plan. Practice what you want to communicate or seek counsel so you can have another perspective. Have a humble approach; developing good communication skills can take time. Be willing to try and be patient. Remember avoiding a problem does not necessarily make it go away.

The eyes of your heavenly Father see and know all things! As flawed human beings, resting our hope on the template formed by other people's lives is risky. We should look unto Jesus, the author and finisher of our faith. In His example, despite our utter rejection of Him, he extends His love, grace and mercy to us every day. His banner over us is truly love. Let us be eager to be the same way!

Proverbs 16:18 "Pride goes before destruction, a haughty spirit before a fall."

John 10:10 "The thief comes only to steal and kill and destroy; I have come that they may have life and have it to the full."

Colossians 3:14 "And over all these virtues put on love, which binds them all together in perfect unity."

Words of Reflection

Chapter 12

I'm Angry, Resentful And Bitter

Having joy can make others around you envious of the sense of freedom, deep happiness, contentment and peace you possess. This feeling is good to pursue, however, harboring constant anger and exuding feelings of resentment toward others is unattractive and will cause people to want to disengage with you. This is not God's will for you. Living in this manner would not be a good representation of your better self. Given the choice, we would prefer to keep whatever happiness we have. Learn to count your blessings, doing so might offer you perspectives that miraculously can cause you to walk in peace.

There may be times when life's assaults can cause us to be angry. Anger is a hurt response—some situations are not fair. For example, you follow the rules, you do your job and still go unnoticed, unappreciated or unrecognized for your efforts. Let the truth as revealed in God's word set you free!

The way stress, trauma or challenging situations impact people can very well justify our anger; however, resentment and bitter emotions need to be treated as toxins within the body and extracted out immediately. When you realize these cancerous, negative emotions, get help. These foreign matters are intruders to your soul. If such emotions are prolonged, they can bring about destruction, more pain, division and disappointment, clouding you and your destiny.

Your soul is not destined to harbor such foreign and toxic imposters. The enemy of your soul wants you to believe that you will be led by these emotions. He is the Father of lies. Do not accept your condition to be something other than that of a child of the King. Surrender to healing. Offer forgiveness, practice patience and love unapologetically.

Job 7:11 "Therefore I will not keep silent; I will speak out in the anguish of my spirit, I will complain in the bitterness of my soul."

Psalm 51:7-10 "Cleanse me with hyssop, and I will be clean; wash me, and I will be whiter than snow. Let me hear joy and gladness; let the bones you have crushed rejoice. Hide your face from my sins and blot out all my iniquity. Create in me a pure heart, O God, and renew a steadfast spirit within me."

Proverbs 3:1 "My son, do not forget my teaching, but keep my commands in your heart."

Words of Reflection

Chapter 13

Helpers Along The Way

People make the world go 'round. The input of cultural dynamics, education, knowledge, ideologies, and diverse experiences, etc. influences us. The plethora of information, especially in this data-driven world can be both challenging and damaging. Hence it is important to have a solid source of truth and for us as children of God that is the Holy Spirit. The Holy Spirit can help you decern in which direction to go. There are YouTube videos, webinars and podcasts serving as teachers offering all sorts of information, tips, suggestions, persuasions, and guidance for every issue under the sun. As revealed in God's word, in the last days, there would be an increase of knowledge, but will the Son of Man find faith?

The Holy Spirit is also called a helper, a guide, a teacher and a leader who hears and relay truth, in today's world it is becoming more and more difficult to decipher godly information from good information, truth from error and the voice of God from the voice of a stranger.

Desire to know the true helper who is the Holy Spirit. He resides in you and will lead you to all truth. Discerning the right voices to listen to and when is priceless. Ask the Holy Spirit to guide you. Put away pride and fear. Pray and exercise humility to learn from those around you with more knowledge and experience.

Isaiah 9:6 "For to us a child is born, to us a son is given, and the government will be on his shoulders. And he will be called Wonderful Counselor, Mighty God, Everlasting Father, Prince of Peace."

Psalm 119:105 "Your word is a lamp for my feet, a light on my path."

Matthew 7:7-8 "Ask and it will be given to you; seek and you will find; knock and the door will be opened to you. For everyone who asks receives; the one who seeks finds; and to the one who knocks, the door will be opened."

Words of Reflection

Chapter 14

A Process Toward Reconciliation

One of the benefits of time is that it can bring perspective and healing. Like time, distance from an unsettling place can encourage reflection. When the fog metaphorically settles on a matter, you can see the situation more clearly. Rehabbing from painful situations can be messy and unpredictable. Some days you will feel strong, and some days you will feel weak. Perseverance is the key. There is more to gain pursuing what is good, righteous and loving.

The goal to heal and be restored in fellowship or unity again with others should stay in view, however, sometimes our process is rushed, and the necessary work needed to grow, mature and heal is aborted prematurely. Being forced to the finish line without forgiveness in the heart from one or both of the affected parties is not wise. Pastors, gurus, counselors or victimizers should indicate when it is time to get over an offense. God can convict the heart. Stay prayerful because there is no magic formula for how long it takes people to get over an offense or grievance.

If you have any urgency, let it be the urgency to desire to please your heavenly Father. He will direct your path. While forgiveness is crucial, and it will be your ticket to setting yourself free, freedom does not always mean reconciliation. It does, however, always lead to peace. A heart ready to reconcile will come in due course. Give yourself permission to fall and get back up. Be gracious with yourself as the Lord is with you. Laugh at your humanity all while journeying forward in obedience.

Psalm 46:10 "He says, 'Be still, and know that I am God; I will be exalted among the nations, I will be exalted in the earth.'"

Ecclesiastes 3:11 "He has made everything beautiful in its time. He has also set eternity in the human heart; yet no one can fathom what God has done from beginning to end."

2 Corinthians 5:18 "All this is from God, who reconciled us to himself through Christ and gave us the ministry of reconciliation."

Words of Reflection

Chapter 15

I Surrender. I Am Going To Cooperate With Your Plan

Some people are naturally drawn to drama; they appear to be in the center of all the action. There are others who live to disappear; they really do not exist, and they avoid confrontations at all costs. Neither one of these character types are worth applauding alone, however, having both traits is wise. Now lies the goal to know when to effectively use them, like Jesus who excelled in both.

There are two old hymnals titled "Trust and Obey" and "I Surrender All." They really should play in our minds like some of these top Spotify hits do because they are like prayers! Let not your aim be to always try to fix others, and at the same time, if you are often the timid, non-confrontational type, work on courage so you can confront people when needed.

Take a pause and break from your typical routine, especially if it has caused you trouble. God could be trying to tell you something. Trust and obey. Surrendering to being and doing good or acting in obedience can lead to transformation. This transformation happens to the whole self—the mind, body, soul and spirit. When you say yes to His will for you, you situate yourself into a tighter grip in His hands. He has all of you now, and that is marvelous. Now, await the day to soar, and believe me, you will journey to joyous days ahead.

Proverbs 18:10 "The name of the Lord is a fortified tower; the righteous run to it and are safe."

Luke 10:41-42 "'Martha, Martha,'" the Lord answered, 'You are worried and upset about many things, but few things are needed—or indeed only one. Mary has chosen what is better, and it will not be taken away from her.'"

John 21:17 "The third time he said to him, 'Simon son of John, do you love me?' Peter was hurt because Jesus asked him the third time, 'Do you love me?' He said, 'Lord, you know all things; you know that I love you.' Jesus said, 'Feed my sheep.'"

Words of Reflection

Chapter 16

Your Presence Is Like A Balm

The world is full of pleasures that cater to our minds and bodies, yet the soul and spirit are often left neglected, getting the short end of the stick. We all have choices. You can light a candle, sit and eat chocolates all day, or sip on fine wine, bury yourself in paperwork, watch another movie or play one more round of video games. Balance time out for these important things and more. Self-care is important, but balance it out with time with God, worship and devotion. The earth is the Lord's and the fullness there is. God created us to enjoy the land.

There is something almost unexplainable that happens when your spirit is well fed. Its power crushes everything foreign in the soul and body. My vision becomes very clear, perspectives are changed, thoughts are more positive and speech is kinder. Your heavenly Father's presence can make you feel whole and joyous. Jesus is still in the healing business. You can trust that God's plan for you is good.

Give it a try. Start with a song, a dance, a poem, or even a cry. Start with being in His presence! Remember your maker as you love yourself

Isaiah 55:1-2 "Come, all you who are thirsty, come to the waters; and you who have no money, come, buy and eat! Come, buy wine and milk without money and without cost. Why spend money on what is not bread, and your labor on what does not satisfy? Listen, listen to me, and eat what is good, and you will delight in the richest of fare.

John 7:38 "Whoever believes in me, as Scripture has said, rivers of living water will flow from within them."

1 John 2:16 "For everything in the world—the lust of the flesh, the lust of the eyes, and the pride of life—comes not from the Father but from the world."

Words of Reflection

Chapter 17

Back To Life, Back To Reality

Utopia does not exist in the world, but should this reality make us despair of righteous living? Of course not! From our vantage point, and as children of God, we have an eternal home, where being in a state of pain, chaos, friction and drama really does not exist, and life there is beyond utopian. It is glorious!

Christ promised us peace and joy, the abundant life that our heavenly Father destined for us to have. A world-changing experience in your life does not, most of the time; change the world around you. We can become the change that we wish to see in others. When we show up healthy, strong, anointed, soulful and ready, we can unashamedly transfer our anointing, inspiration, talents and influence onto others.

There are people you've been destined to impact for God's glory. Be gracious and forgiving with yourself. Practice right doing and stay committed to truth. Believe in God's word and have confidence in faith because it works. The reality is you are an overcomer.

Deuteronomy 30:19 "This day I call the heavens and the earth as witnesses against you that I have set before you life and death, blessings and curses. Now choose life, so that you and your children may live."

John 16:33 "I have told you these things, so that in me you may have peace. In this world you will have trouble. But take heart! I have overcome the world."

Ephesians 6:12 "For our struggle is not against flesh and blood, but against the rulers, against the authorities, against the powers of this dark world and against the spiritual forces of evil in the heavenly realms."

Words of Reflection

Chapter 18

Your Love, O'lord, Is Amazing

Acts of love are worth showing off! Here is a tribute to Love…..true love reveals itself. It is not shameful, neither is it bashful. Love is bold and it is passionate. Laws cannot seem to regulate it. Like sweet-smelling perfume, love can envelop you in all the right places and melt hardness away. Like tickling a child, love makes you smile on the inside. It sparks excitement and can cause you to dream in bold living color.

Did you know love is also smart and intelligent? Yes, it can really blow your mind away! God loves. He speaks a language that we can understand. And he is inviting you to deeper places and higher heights, where there is an overwhelming sensation of joy. Your soul cannot contain it. So, if you're in a hurtful or challenging relationships ask the Lord to blanket you with his love. Wait for it, you will know, feel and experience its power.

Repeat after me: I was created by love, so I can love and be loved by others.

Romans 8:39 "Neither height nor depth, nor anything else in all creation, will be able to separate us from the love of God that is in Christ Jesus our Lord."

1 John 4:8 "Whoever does not love does not know God, because God is love."

1 John 4:19 "We love because he first loved us."

Words of Reflection

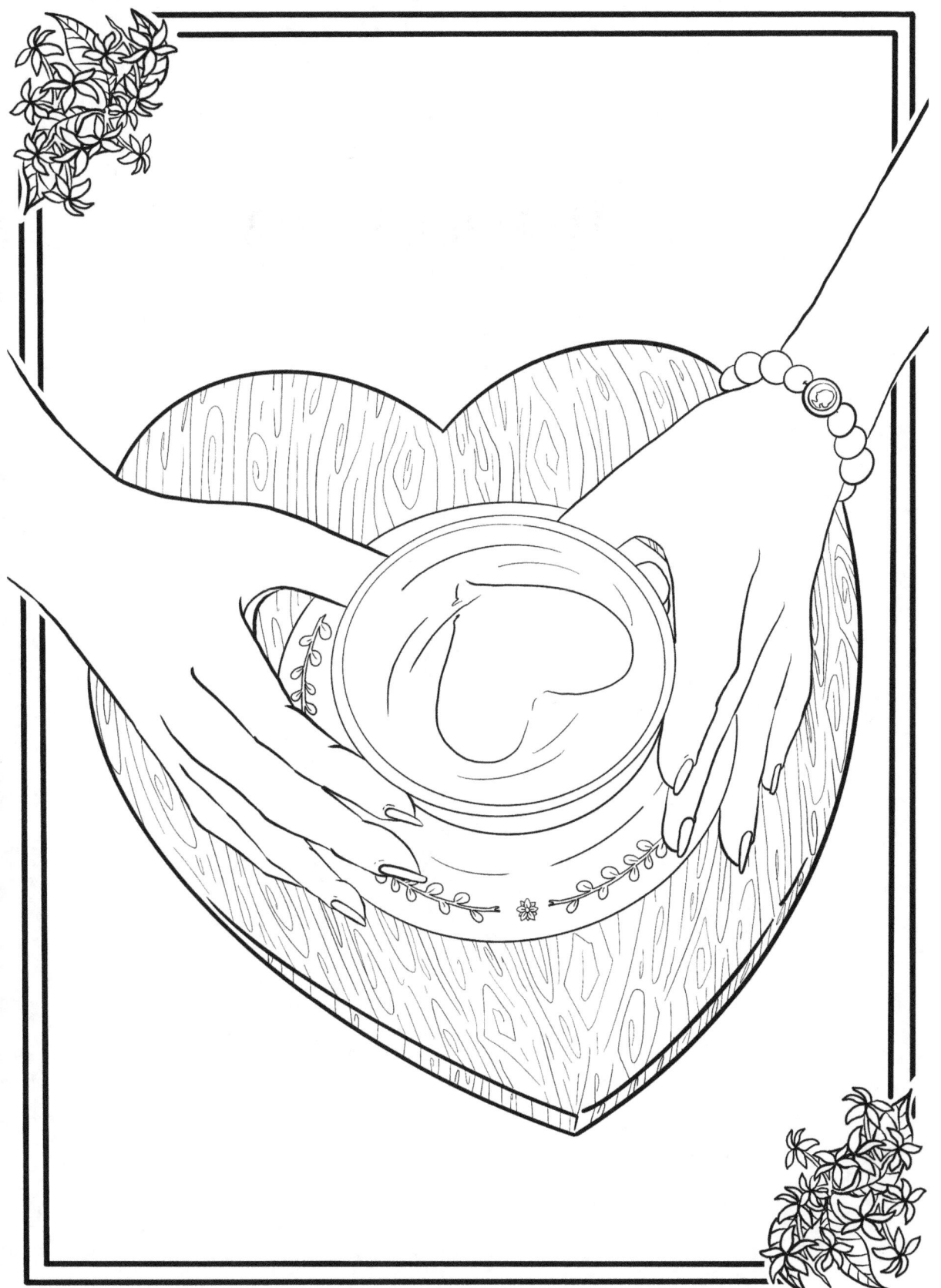

Chapter 19

It Didn't Turn Out As Planned. Now What?

Judas betrayed Jesus with a kiss. Being full of love and purpose, Jesus continued with His mission. Later, Judas felt sorry for betraying His Lord, and went off to take his own life, a cowardly act certainly. Judas' sorrow leads to death. Jesus on the other hand, despite the betrayal, pursued love, truth and commitment. His obedience resulted in life for all who would believe in Him.

The reality is some people will turn into you, and you both may get a chance to journey in this life harmoniously with them. There are times when people will turn away from you and not want to return. Do not let anyone deter you from your mission and purpose. Judgment for all lies in the hands of our heavenly Father. Trust Him to carry you through.

Your life was planned since you were in your mother's womb. Do not underestimate the power of destiny and fate. Let God your heavenly Father light your path and guide your footsteps. Your plan may appear to be working and then it all fails, but in hindsight, if you look to God, you will see his handiwork in ordering your footsteps for your good throughout your journey.

Psalm 3:3 "But you, Lord, are a shield around me, my glory, the One who lifts my head high."

Matthew 18:21 "Then Peter came to Jesus and asked, 'Lord, how many times shall I forgive my brother or sister who sins against me? Up to seven times?' Jesus answered, 'I tell you, not seven times, but seventy-seven times.'"

Romans 11:29 "For God's gifts and his call are irrevocable."

Words of Reflection

Chapter 20

Look At Me! I Feel Like I Have Wings!

There are events in life that we thought would knock us out, but instead, they only made us stronger, wiser, more thoughtful, more giving and more considerate.

Do you realize that what happens to you does not have to own you? You have a beautiful soul and were created to be pure. Emotions like sadness, disappointment and anger can serve as simple reminders or warning signs from the soul. When the alarm goes off, go to your quiet place and have a "checkout with the Holy Spirit." There is no need to invite panic, worry or negativity into your mind and heart. Light and darkness cannot cohabitate. You are like a flower; you can radiate beauty. You are like a jewel; you have value. You are like a fine tool; you are purposeful.

You are a child of God, rising to overcome and soar. I remember, so I look up. Have a heart of gratitude, and be content with how far you've come. Despite what launching pad you have in your mind, you are still blessed beyond comprehension.

Deuteronomy 32:10 "In a desert land he found him, in a barren and howling waste. He shielded him and cared for him; he guarded him as the apple of his eye."

Psalm 126: 5-6 "Those who sow with tears, will reap with songs of joy. Those who go out weeping, carrying seed to sow, will return with songs of joy, carrying sheaves with them."

Habakkuk 3:19 "The Sovereign Lord is my strength; He makes my feet like the feet of a deer; He enables me to tread on the heights."

Words of Reflection

About the Author

Jandre

Jandre considers herself a privileged daughter and creative servant of the Lord. In this inaugural edition of her book birthed after having overcome many life challenges, Jandre shares ways after experiencing hurt and pain in relationships one can heal and rebound through scripture meditation and coloring.

Jandre has been graced to wear many hats as wife, mother, sister, servant, and business professional, experiencing God through many joyous and painful encounters herself she is eager to make Him known. Her many talents have enabled her to be in institutional and church leadership, serve in administration, lead music encourager, committed intercessory prayer leader and a creative professional. She enjoys meeting people and encouraging them to "taste and see the Lord's goodness for themselves".

Jandre also works as a business professional, using her administrative skills to serve in the marketplace. In her spare time, she manages the "The One Line Of Encouragement" social media group on the WhatsApp platform. Her hobbies include dancing, journal writing, cooking, coordinating "something" and prayer- a true testament to where her inspiration and strength comes from.

Jandre resides in in Boston, MA and is married to her "chosen one," her spouse for over 20 years. Together they have two beautiful teenage daughters that are blossoming beautifully in God's grace and mercy.

www.ingramcontent.com/pod-product-compliance
Lightning Source LLC
Chambersburg PA
CBHW081157070526
44583CB00021B/2887